Life-Changing Classics, Volume III

A MESSAGE TO
GARCIA

Elbert Hubbard

**Executive
Books**

Life-Changing Classics, Volume III
A Message to Garcia

Published by
Executive Books
206 West Allen Street
Mechanicsburg, PA 17055

Introduction by Jason Liller
Cover by David Bullock/Susquehanna Direct

ISBN: 0-937539-65-1

Printed in the United States of America

Contents

Introduction

Andrew Summers Rowan, the inspiration for this small masterpiece, carried his famous message to Cuban insurgent leader Calixco Garcia y Ignigues during America's war with Spain—and received the distinguished service cross for his effort.

Born in 1857 in Monroe County, Virginia (now West Virginia), Rowan graduated from West Point in 1881 and spent a number of years with the U.S. Army Information Bureau in Central America. He was still a lieutenant when he was called upon to render service in Cuba.

Afterwards, he continued to serve during the Philippine insurrection, held posts at several military bases in the U.S. and taught military science and tactics at Kansas State Agriculture College.

Col. Andrew S. Rowan

Colonel Rowan retired in 1909 and spent the remainder of his years in San Francisco, where he died in 1943. The service that he offered his country was beyond reproach and a grateful nation offered its recognition. His greatest contribution, however, was almost certainly the inspiration that he unknowingly provided to Elbert Hubbard who immortalized the story of his daring mission to Cuba in *A Message to Garcia*, for it is through this modest essay that Colonal Rowan has influenced the lives of countless millions.

Apologia

This literary trifle, *A Message To Garcia*, was written one evening after supper, in a single hour. It was on the 22nd of February, 1899, Washington's Birthday: we were just going to press with the March *Philistine*.

The thing leaped hot from my heart, written after a trying day, when I had been endeavoring to train some rather delinquent villagers to abjure the comatose state and get radioactive.

The immediate suggestion, though, came from a little argument over the teacups, when my boy Bert suggested that Rowan was the real hero of the Cuban War. Rowan had gone alone and done the thing—carried the message to Garcia.

It came to me like a flash! Yes, the boy is right, the hero is the man who does his work—who carries the message to Garcia. I got up from the table, and wrote *A Message To Garcia*. I thought so little of it that we ran it in the magazine without a heading. The edition went out, and soon orders began to come for extra copies of the March *Philistine*, a dozen, fifty, a hundred, and when the American News Company ordered a thousand, I asked one of my helpers which article it was that stirred up the cosmic dust. "It's the stuff about Garcia," he said.

The next day a telegram came from George H. Daniels, of the New York Central Railroad thus, "Give price on one hundred thousand Rowan article in pamphlet form—Empire State Express advertisement on back—also how soon can ship."

I replied giving price, and stated we could supply the pamphlets in two years. Our facilities were small and a hundred thousand booklets looked like an awful undertaking.

The result was that I gave Mr. Daniels permission to reprint the article in his own way. He issued it in booklet form in editions of half a million. Two or three of these half-million lots were sent out by Mr. Daniels, and in addition the article was reprinted in over two hundred magazines and newspapers. It has been translated into all written languages.

At the time Mr. Daniels was distributing *A Message To Garcia*, Prince Hilakoff, Director of Russian Railways, was in this country. He was the guest of the New York Central, and made a tour of the country under the personal direction of Mr. Daniels. The Prince saw the little book and was interested in it, more because Mr. Daniels was putting it out in big numbers, probably, than otherwise. In any event, when he got home he had the matter translated into Russian, and a copy of the booklet given to every railroad employee in Russia.

Other countries then took it up, and from Russia it passed into Germany, France, Spain, Turkey, Hindustan and China. During the war between Russia and Japan, every Russian soldier who went to the front was given a copy of *A Message To Garcia*. The Japanese, finding the booklets in possession of the Russian prisoners, concluded it must be a good thing, and accordingly translated it into Japanese.

And on an order of the Mikado, a copy was given to every man in the employ of the Japanese Government, soldier or civilian. Over forty million copies of *A Message To Garcia* have been printed. This is said to be a larger circulation than any other literary venture has ever attained during the lifetime of an author, in all history—thanks to a series of lucky accidents.

E.H.

East Aurora,
December 1, 1913

Words of Elbert Hubbard...

The best preparation for tomorrow's work is to do your work as well as you can today.

* * * * * * * *

If you work for a man,
For God's sake, work for him.
If he pays you your bread and butter,
Think well of him, speak well of him.

* * * * * * * *

Get your Happiness out of your work or you will never know what Happiness is.

* * * * * * * *

The mintage of wisdom
Is to know that rest is rust,
And that REAL LIFE
Is in love, laughter, and work.

* * * * * * * *

Folks who never do any more than they get paid for, never get paid for any more than they do.

The hero is the man who forgets himself for others.

— Soldier's Testament

A Message to Garcia

In all this **Cuban business** there is one man stands out on the horizon of my memory like Mars at perihelion.

When war broke out between Spain and the United States it was very necessary to communicate quickly with the leader of the Insurgents. Garcia was somewhere in the mountain vastness of Cuba—no one knew where. No mail nor telegraph message could reach him. The President must secure his cooperation, and quickly. What to do!

Someone said to the President, "There's a fellow by the name of Rowan will find Garcia for you, if anybody can."

Rowan was sent for and given a letter to be delivered to Garcia. How "the fellow by the name of Rowan" took the letter, sealed it up in an oil-skin pouch, strapped it

Duty

*Those who preach duty and
whine about it are to be pitied because they
do not know that duty is borne of
love. Duty carries its own beatitude,
its call is a fanfare of trumpets. So it
is with the humblest of men in war,
and so should mortal virtue be.*

— Soldier's Testament

over his heart, in four days landed by night off the coast of Cuba from an open boat, disappeared into the jungle, and in three weeks came out on the other side of the Island, having traversed a hostile country on foot, and delivered his letter to Garcia—are things I have no special desire now to tell in detail. The point that I wish to make is this: McKinley gave Rowan a letter to be delivered to Garcia; Rowan took the letter and did not ask, "Where is he at?"

By the Eternal! there is a man whose form should be cast in deathless bronze and the statue placed in every college of the land. It is not book-learning young men need, nor instruction about this and that, but a stiffening of the vertebrae which will cause them to be loyal to a trust, to act promptly, concentrate their energies: do the thing—"Carry a message to Garcia!"

General Garcia is dead now, but there are other Garcias. No man who has endeavored to carry out an enterprise where many hands were needed, but has been wellnigh appalled at times by the imbecility of

The man who revels in difficulties is the man who knows he can surmount them.

**— Soldier's
Testament**

the average man—the inability or unwilling-ness to concentrate on a thing and do it.

Slipshod assistance, foolish inatten-tion, dowdy indifference, and half-hearted work seem the rule; and no man succeeds, unless by hook or crook or threat he forces or bribes other men to assist him; or mayhap, God in His goodness performs a miracle, and sends him an Angel of Light for an assistant.

You, reader, put this matter to a test: You are sitting now in your office—six clerks are within call. Summon any one and make this request: "Please look in the ency-clopedia and make a brief memorandum for me concerning the life of Correggio." Will the clerk quietly say, "Yes, sir," and go do the task?

On your life, he will not. He will look at you out of a fishy eye and ask one or more of the following questions:

Who was he?

The man who gives himself wholly and disinterestedly in a crisis need never be ashamed of himself, even if he is mistaken.

— *Soldier's Testament*

Which encyclopedia?

Where is the encyclopedia?

Was I hired for that?

Don't you mean Bismarck?

What's the matter with Charlie doing it?

Is he dead?

Is there any hurry?

Sha'n't I bring you the book and let you look it up yourself?

What do you want to know for?

And I will lay you ten to one that after you have answered the questions, and explained how to find the information, and why you want it, the clerk will go off and get one of the other clerks to help him try to find Garcia—and then come back and tell you there is no such man. Of course I may lose my bet, but according to the Law of

> *Audacity may seem foolish to those who shrink back, but it is the only possible course for those who are capable of looking ahead.*
>
> *— Soldier's Testament*

Average, I will not.

Now, if you are wise, you will not bother to explain to your "assistant" that Correggio is indexed under the C's, not in the K's, but you will smile very sweetly and say, "Never mind," and go look it up yourself. And this incapacity for independent action, this moral stupidity, this infirmity of the will, this unwillingness to cheerfully catch hold and lift—these are the things that put pure Socialism so far into the future. If men will not act for themselves, what will they do when the benefit of their effort is for all?

A first-mate with knotted club seems necessary; and the dread of getting "the bounce" Saturday night holds many a worker to his place. Advertise for a stenographer, and nine out of ten who apply can neither spell nor punctuate—and do not think it necessary to.

Can such a one write a letter to Garcia?

All men envy courage, even those who belittle it.

— Soldier's Testament

"You see that bookkeeper," said the foreman to me in a large factory.

"Yes, what about him?"

"Well he's a fine accountant, but if I'd send him up town on an errand, he might accomplish the errand all right, and on the other hand, might stop at four saloons on the way, and when he got to Main Street would forget what he had been sent for." Can such a man be entrusted to carry a message to Garcia?

We have recently been hearing much maudlin sympathy expressed for the "down-trodden denizens of the sweat-shop" and the "homeless wanderer searching for honest employment," and with it all often go many hard words for the men in power.

Nothing is said about the employer who grows old before his time in a vain attempt to get frowsy ne'er-do-wells to do intelligent work; and his long, patient striving after "help" that does nothing but loaf when his back is turned.

Impartiality is only a virtue in small men. In men of greater stature it is a weakness and a vice. It means that they lack the capacity to support the rigors of a high destiny.

— *Soldier's Testament*

In every store and factory there is a constant weeding-out process going on. The employer is constantly sending away "help" that have shown their incapacity to further the interests of the business, and others are being taken on. No matter how good times are, this sorting continues: only, if times are hard and work is scarce, the sorting is done finer—but out and forever out the incompetent and unworthy go. It is the survival of the fittest. Self-interest prompts every employer to keep the best—those who can carry a message to Garcia.

I know one man of really brilliant parts who has not the ability to manage a business of his own, and yet who is absolutely worthless to any one else, because he carries with him constantly the insane suspicion that his employer is oppressing, or intending to oppress, him. He cannot give orders; and he will not receive them. Should a message be given him to take to Garcia, his answer would probably be, "Take it yourself!"

Tonight this man walks the streets looking for work, the wind whistling

The brave man's body is never too exhausted to respond to his demands upon it. It always has a last reserve.

— Soldier's Testament

through his threadbare coat. No one who knows him dare employ him, for he is a regular firebrand of discontent. He is impervious to reason, and the only thing that can impress him is the toe of a thick-soled Number Nine boot.

Of course I know that one so morally deformed is no less to be pitied than a physical cripple; but in our pitying, let us drop a tear, too, for the men who are striving to carry on a great enterprise, whose working hours are not limited by the whistle, and whose hair is fast turning white through the struggle to hold in line dowdy indifference, slipshod imbecility, and the heartless ingratitude which, but for their enterprise, would be both hungry and homeless.

Have I put the matter too strongly? Possibly I have; but when all the world has gone a-slumming I wish to speak a word of sympathy for the man who succeeds—the man who, against great odds, has directed the efforts of others, and having succeeded, finds there's nothing in it: nothing but bare board and clothes. I have carried a dinner

*It is our duty to judge ourselves
more severely than men judge us.
Whatever men say of you,
whatever they do to you,
always remain serene and unangered.
Seen in the quiet mind,
those words which fly so wildly
will only bear their just weight.
Evil hours should be passed
in the silence of Gethsemane.
Turn your eyes upon Me and do not fret
about the judgments of the world,
for your peace of mind
is not at the mercy of the tongues of men.
Whatever they may think of you,
you can be nothing but what you are,
and where can abide peace, truth and glory
if not in Me?*

— Soldier's Testament

pail and worked for day's wages, and I have also been an employer of labor, and I know there is something to be said on both sides.

There is no excellence, per se, in poverty; rags are no recommendation; and all employers are not rapacious and high-handed, any more than all poor men are virtuous. My heart goes out to the man who does his work when the "boss" is away, as well as when he is at home. And the man who, when given a letter for Garcia, quietly takes the missive, without asking any idiotic questions, and with no lurking intention of chucking it into the nearest sewer, or of doing aught else but deliver it, never gets "laid off" nor has to go on a strike for higher wages.

Civilization is one long anxious search for just such individuals. Anything such a man asks shall be granted. He is wanted in every city, town and village—in every office, shop, store and factory. The world cries out for such: he is needed and needed badly—the man who can "Carry a Message to Garcia."

About Elbert Hubbard

**E**lbert Hubbard was born in 1859 in Bloomington, Illinois, and never received more than a grade-school education. A self-made man in many respects, Hubbard filled in the gaps in his knowledge through voracious reading, a passion which became manifest in the founding of the Roycroft Shop, a publishing house specializing in deluxe bindings. He wrote a series of 182 biographies under the series title *Little Journeys to Homes of the Great* and also published two magazines, *The Philistine* and *The Fra*, producing much of the content himself.

Elbert Hubbard and his wife, Alice, were traveling to England on the Lusitania and went down with the ship when it was struck by a German torpedo on May 7th, 1915.